IMMORTALITY

IMMORTALITY
INHALED FEELINGS, EXHALED CREATIVITY

YARA ALKHALID

PARTRIDGE

To order additional copies of this book, contact
Toll Free 800 101 2657 (Singapore)
Toll Free 1 800 81 7340 (Malaysia)
orders.singapore@partridgepublishing.com

www.partridgepublishing.com/singapore

Author's Bio

Hello,

My name is Yara Alkhalid; I'm 20 years old, I'm from Riyadh- Saudi Arabia and I'm medical student.

I've always had a dream of being an official writer with my own book, I was only waiting for the potentials to crash my path hopefully one day, yet I never realized that the potentials was right between my palms and I'm the one who gets to walk through it till I reach what I had always wanted.

I started writing all types of poetries since I was 12 years old and have always painted in my little mind that held a wild imagination that one day I'll publish a book.

Never give up!

A very special thanks goes to my friend Ghada Faisal who is a very talented artist, I handled her the responsibility of the cover because I trust her talent 100%, and she's the one who made the cover design

You can check her work on her account on instagram:
@ninettyseven

For any more details or, suggestion don't hesitate:
Twitter: @Yara2k
Instagram: @Yara2k.lines
Email: <u>yara.alkhalid@yahoo.com</u>

Syllables:

1-thank you mom
2-thank you dad
3- something to last
4-that conversation
5-infinite trace
6-essential glass
7-behind the blocks
8-beautiful nightmare
9-coal vs. diamonds
10- hour after hour
11-your point of view
12-what lasts?
13-after all
14- behind that
15-incomplete
16-seek for better
17- what if life was from our imagination
18-3AM glasses
19- I let you
20- we can build an empire
21- out of words
22-out of words
23-precious value

24-united

25-crowded place

26-it used to be a mystery

27-frost

28-change

29- definition by the cover

30-steady flight

31-winter nights in July

32-isolation

33-no and not

34-released

35-A good reason

36- something true

37-they don't understand

38-someone you'll enjoy

39-misunderstood

40-immortality

"THANK YOU, MOM"

I came to this life as a dream to her,

A dream came true.

Since I came to this life, this dream has transferred into me.

That, I wanted her to see happiness right through

I wanted to paint her black edges in blue.

In her smile,

I see the life that I can't imagine it without her by my side.

I have a lot of flaws that she wish that I exist without it,

Here I am embracing it out of the traditional way.

I know she hides so much by lying and expressing the okay,

And I know I can't make it fade.

But for a minute I'll let it sway.

For an hour, I'll wear it, as something I weigh,

And I hope the storm will blow it away.

To god I'll pray, That I will never taste a day without her.

"THANK YOU, DAD"

A shelter to the harm,

Every time I was about to fell, he was the alarm.

He saw his illusions in me,

And I figured out that it was disillusions, yet he created a hope.

He struggled, but to his potential I was a dope.

He wanted me to achieve,

That was his only way to feel relieved.

He has beliefs,

By pushing me forward to what I was afraid of

Right when I was about to leave,

To leave his dreamy mind

For living, I thought I was naïve

But, now I'm here to redeem your grieves.

To rise your head up, not making you regret that I was here,

Brighten my name to your ears.

You don't have to be afraid to check a seer,

I'm here to make everything clear,

Because Without you, I'm weak,

And without your potentials in me, I leak.

"Something to Last"

There goes a knife,
You Feel like a widow yet still a wife,
Shredded days till the after life.
Not a steady king,
A bird with no wings,
Teary vocal cords,
Sad songs to sing,
The blood is covering everything,
Not making you notice what you've caused,
But there's a sparkle outside.
Chances can ring,
A sound in the inside,
Want you to hear it before it dies,
Instead of fragile shelter you'll provide,
Echoes of a satisfaction,
There will never be expiration on our pride.
Things might seem hard,
Things might fall apart,
But from this we can start.
The union of hope and passion drains from
the heart.
Paint a shade
With an infinite marker,

Life doesn't have a grade.
Memories aren't only something we've made,
Not something our time period have weighed,
It's the faith outcome
It's a blade,
A blade that we have learned from
Let's leave, but in immortality way.
Don't strangle your name in oblivion.
Let's make the others tomorrows our yesterday,
Because we have never actually left
People still mention us when they pray.
Create the others steps when they're halfway.
Be the immorality,
Not fragile clay,
And that's why I wrote this.
I imagine what's next,
Nothing to miss,
Unique personality,
Virtues of originality,
I leave this life with a mark not just a shade,
I'm the immortality.

"THAT CONVERSATION"

In a sparkly night,
Beside a candle light
Where their thoughts climbed.
He said, "Faking is the worst crime."
She asked, "Why are you dressed up like that this time?"
He said, "It would impress his friends."
So she nodded saying, "then you deserve a fine,
That is nothing but a pretend."
He said," I would never use a person to bend."
She said "but you might fall to where you extend,
And that's where you'll need a depend,
Someone for your greed they'll defend,
Because every lonely person has an end,
Instead of paying for shadows bills."
He said, "but every shadow will disappear when the moon appears"
She replayed, "What is the use of a world without your parents near?
Even if they couldn't be there for the next year,

But their scent is descendant and clear."
He said, "some people have reached the top
like they were able to touch the atmosphere."
She said, "That happens when you're ready
to transform your fears,
Leave them aside as a souvenir or a strength
cheer."
So, the daylight came,
And her shadow disappeared
Where he was standing right beside the
lake,
Where he was using god as a purpose for
his sake,
Where he stood he was ready for every
break,
Collide a lesson into a mistake
Where he was finally awake,
Where he promised himself
He'll be the reason for humanity earthquake.
He said,
"I'm ready unconditionally,
I'm ready under any circumstance.
Thank you, god
She was a hope to this chance
She gave me a better life glance".

"Infinite Trace"

When our dreams turned nothing, but a
hope.
It's like we're strangled with a rope,
No way out of this lope,
And our fears became nothing, but a dope.
That girl in a middle of nowhere,
She came in the dawn,
She was breathing a fresh air,
And ours were filled with smoke.
With her frizzy hair,
Her feet were also bare,
She said with a delightful glance,
"Time is another word for new chance,
Never freeze it unless your soul freezes
everything."
We thought with our fears and injured
smiles,
That we were loyal to our consciences, when
we were only betrayers,
But we have never realized that we can still
edit our files.
That from our goals, we were close
Just a little walk to reset our miles

We were the only cause of our broken bones.
We weren't able to reach,
We could have painted our lives with colors,
But we choose to bleach.
We were drowning in illusions of fairytales
We recognized our hearts as a fragile glass,
While some got out of it with only broken
nails
We focused on the image,
And forgot the details,
Because we forgot that challenges also
could end in fails.
We focused on who has left and stayed,
What is actually real won't find no excuse
to be here.
In a very great distance
Will always be near.
Our dreams were like the moon, far.
And our rocket ships was about to touch it,
Until we got lost in space,
I realized that by only staring at her smile
with her naked feet.
She left an infinite trace.
My life is not about whom I meet,
To my starve I'm the only treat
To my cold I'm the only heat,
I get to change the gloomy streets.
And where do I take seats,

That girl has raised the concrete.
That girl with nothing felt complete,
While we had everything,
But our inner organs
Felt empty.

"ESSENTIAL GLASS"

As you get older,
The world gets colder.
Things used to be bright,
But the gold must find a way to become stainless.
Bleeding acceleration hurts so much for the first time,
But when we get used to it, it starts to feel painless.
People starts to remove their Halloween masks,
And the common thing between them and this celebration that they remain evil
So, we hear every single day the sound of a broken flask.
Everything seems difficult not as our life primeval.
Lessons are learned,
We start to recognize what should be heard,
True or fake people that their backs have turned,
But that's the part in life where we get stronger.

We fall,
And first we start using a wheel chair to heal,
We were small
Secondly, we use a clutch to stand,
How beautiful the world is when we're standing tall.
The curves are vanishing and we start using our legs back,
Weak people only gets to crawl,
But we shouldn't,
Because everyone was born for a reason
As blurry the vision was,
It gets clearer by every season.
We were created in this life with a spot,
Either we reach it or watch someone else become essential.

"BEHIND THE BLOCKS"

Exposing thoughts till we drain
Karma is our deeds
Try to reverse the word deed,
And that is where it will come back to you,
And when we rush things in speed,
Try to reverse the word speed and you'll get
where you'll fall,
You'll fall in deeps
And in deep where our feelings hunt us,
And we run to exceed.
Pain is our creativity fuel,
And behind it a hidden jewel,
But every eye will find a moment,
A moment to merge with a star
Short road or far,
But we'll embrace who we are
And one day your smile will heal someone's
scar,
Because there's always a beauty behind a
broken jar

Poetry will remain speechless,
Where the widow will turn into a wife.
Life can have smoother blade of a knife
Dead heart will come back to life.

"Beautiful nightmare"

Let me tell you a story
Better than Romeo and Juliet
That's the real history, that's a glory
That's the best thing I could ever get.
Trying to think of someone else
I couldn't, I'm sorry.
I tried to think straight,
But it's like I've been punched with a lorry.
I'm walking half blind,
Because I was walking without you,
Until I found your eyes,
Where I turned completely blind,
Yet I realized I was a genius,
Until I've lost my mind
Loving you.
Never realized how skies could be that blue.
My un sleep sweet dreams,
My soiree sparks,
I had doubts in angel's existence till I found
you in my stream.
It's like a shark has bitten me,
In a thousand of grudges we have found a
way for them to be settled.

I found you as glees,
A beautiful snake nettle,
And I'll promise you this:
I'll be your escape when you're about to explode.
Whenever you lost your way back home, I'll be your road.
Don't make me face this world alone.
When you get injured, I'll be your remedy.
I'll be whatever you need,
Just don't turn this into a memory.
I wish I could describe you in words, but that's hard
Because I'm your gamble and you're my devious,
Because you're the wish that I crave
Your voice was a bandage when I was about to break.
Your smile scent even if it's actually fake.
With you, my path of happiness ends and starts
My love for you beats from the heart.

"COAL VS. DIAMONDS"

Sometimes it's a diamond
And sometimes it's a coal,
The way you treat my heart.
Sometimes it's a breath taking
Sometimes you break us apart
The way you treat my heart.
So, I closed my eyes
It's way better to think about you there,
Because over there I know that there are
no lies,
Only in my isolated imagination
We used to have a strong nation.
I got drunk in tears,
I taste this salty water every single night.
And I hold our future in fears,
Can't control your sight.
Hurting me has became an art
Darling, you're so creative.
I should have left from the start,
But I became numb in love
Never used my mind, not so smart,
Because you are really half part,
Half part of my soul, or even my whole soul

You're asleep,
And I'm wide-awake in the dawn.
It feels too far
I couldn't taste the yawns,
I'm lost all night.
It feels so clear that you complete me.
My heart has been always covered with dust,
While it was clean when you filled me with emotions and lived there,
But I walked with your shoe when your legs were broken.
I've been strangled with lots of things that I left it unspoken.
Lots of energy in me has been stolen,
Lots of love without my permission has been stolen.
Sharp nights with you, but I don't know how you're every atom in my air,
The reason behind every chemical bound in my body.
I should have been aware,
But if you actually lasted like this I'll drown,
Because I forgot the ways to sail alone
And also, because you're aura was much more than the oxygen I breath.

"Hour after Hour"

Hour after hour,
I'm fading
Losing all the power,
And the sugar you left on my smile
Taste sour.
Day after day,
I'm waiting,
Shall I stay?
It just taking too long
No words to say,
It's been weeks
Knees so shiver
Bones turned weak
Memories drifting down the river
Red skin, hard to turn my cheek,
But if thoughts can be delivered
Would it change everything?
Thought that I was every reason to seek,
But yeah it's been weeks
Too much to discover behind those eyes
I should look at tomorrow,
But I'm checking if it's possible for
counterclockwise

To get every broken piece in you I would go for any enterprise.
All spider nets will eventually catch butterflies.
Lost the ending to analyze,
Yet I had you in my past
And I can see my future in nobody, but you.
Love for life, love that last
I want to bring our memories back to life, not to view.
Walking through every gloomy avenue,
Looking for what went wrong to review,
A solution or a clue,
But they say the seashore looks scary at night
Not always blue,
But I'll walk in your steps to reach you
Even if it's tight, even with a dirty shoe
Lies is uncovered honesty,
Lies is a shelter for what's true,
Lies are a lot but what we had was clear and few,
And what's real will always find a way out.
Down to the storm, we'll come through.
You complete me, no doubt
I know you can feel me
I know you can hear me even with a silent shout.

"YOUR POINT OF VIEW"

I threw the weight on my shoulder by hurting her,

But she was still there

Trying to calm me down every single time.

She made me bleed sparks,

By watching those softs words come out of her injured lips.

I ignored her, thought that was a solution to my hard times,

But she was there waiting for me.

I asked her, "Why haven't you escaped this war?"

She replied,

"I wanted to be the only one who's surviving."

She had a glass smile that I broke a thousands of times,

But she never stopped bringing the broken pieces in shape,

With her bleeding fingers of the glass blade, And that's where I realized that every broken piece in her

Meant the world to me.

For the first time, I watched her tears streamed down her face,

Because I told her,

I love her...

"WHAT LASTS?"

Does anything in this world last?
Does anything actually last real?
Why deja vu turn my present into past?
How does joy actually feels?
My inner parts can't be described,
Because the words are left in the silence
Do I still get to choose my ways or it's
already prescribed?
Ecstasy and sorrows violence
People says, "I'm stubborn"
So I reply, "it's better than being a follower
You get to choose your own color; Life is not
painted in auburn.
With principles we're not hollowed."
And that's where I proved what they said.
Your pride comes first,
Even if I prefer honesty,
Though I think acting hurts,
And lies are the worst,
And I'm losing this someone in thirst,
But I would rather pretend
It never bothered

Than losing myself into someone who haven't
The echoes of betrayers
Feelings are the equipment for players,
Blood surveyors.
Your mind and time has been deceiving,
Black conveyors
Only slight people are leaving,
But pain is a lesson
And Lesson should be achieved,
Yet when I laugh hard people say I hide behind it tears.
Who said if I smiled I'm grieving?
The strongest trait having fears,
Because of conquering them for your own dreams
My mom once said, "reverse a rumor and you'll get the actual meaning."
People who spread them are secret admires
Slipped shoes, because of clean floor,
That's when you get for whom you'll be leaning.
People are leaving
So, keep your pride and dignity because they have never left.
The moment that you're starving
And you swallowed your grudges
A lot of judges

Ignoring these can be filled with drudges,
But that's where strength and confidence
collide
Anger toward haters has died
Mind has length and wide
Holding your position and your best friend
side
More power from the inside
In result, a smile on feeling satisfied.

"After All"

Let's play hide and seek,
You've been hiding behind my smile,
Your name slips in me.
My heart is so sleek.
You hide behind every word that I speak.
Never knew how conquers feel like,
But with you I've reached the peak.
Your laugh got me on my knees.
One clear symptom, I've became that weak,
Yet when it's my turn to hide,
Your time has been betraying me
Your mind has been deceiving me,
Freedom wants to risk my soul free
I know trust is not for guarantee,
But overland and overseas
You're the only one who owns that key.
Skim through me even for a brief,
You'll not be able to climb again
A punishment for a thief
You'll get even deeper
A wet eraser for the grief
Happiness to pursue,
And If I'm lost in you

Wish black and white would fade in blue,
But they say the tomb can't fit two,
Yet with your touch the memories grew
And that's where I knew
I'm still lingered on the seconds around you.
I have let you drink my tears when you were thirsty
Never let you figure that I was thirsty too.
They immediately remember you when they call my name,
It merges so well.
Life is about give to gain the same,
But the sound of it burns in flame.
It taste sweet, never healthy like an aspartame,
But I have also written you as an aim.
My smile is wide,
As the depth of my pain shelter,
I'm always on your side.
As I promised of the warmth I'll provide,
While I'm freezing in the inside
Burn the cold in your chest,
Push the dignity aside,
Forget the meaning of pride,
Open the things that I hide,
Let your time divide,
I'll let you drive with a delightful ride,
While I'm on the passenger side.

"Behind That"

I overdose you close
Thought this drug would last,
Thought I'll never broke
I'm addicted, how did it finish this fast?
But they say, "the thing we want it the most to last
Will eventually remain in the past."
And the other half of the crowd says,
"The rain will never appear without seeing an overcast."
Like a five years old who just passed a toy store,
I want you.
Like a 13 years old who got sick of advices,
Searching for the easy way of living,
I need you.
Lost myself and that's where I found you.
Like 70 years old who needs a clutch to stand,
Hold me still.
My spectrum is bleaching,
My inner organs are bleeding
You got attracted in the crowd

You forgot that your mind and time has been deceiving.
I'm behind waiting for you,
Waiting for your eyes to catch the corner of mine,
The corner of me sheltering my tears,
The corner of fake dignity I showed you.
You thought I held strength, but that's where it vanished around you.
Haven't they taught you to never judge the book by the view?
Because behind that corner a weakness of love
I'll be there waiting, because behind a world of lies I felt something true.
I'll never be a memory residue,
Because I know my happiness is behind those eyes
And if it wasn't there
Then behind your smile.

"INCOMPLETE"

Shadow covers people's personality

One situation knocks them down.

The sky is full of stars,

I still wonder why do they call it a gloomy town?

Grudges have filled their jars,

While we can use it for flowers

Goals are so far,

And accidents may ruin their cars.

The bright side seems to them so bizarre,

Fears circulate their arteries,

But remember

How the ecstasy taste after being broken.

Join the completed aims and be a proud member.

Join integrity with words plainspoken.

Create warmth in the middle of December.

Even if the majority of the world is glass,

Be the variety and transform into oaken.

Show people the escape of the worst impasse

Even with bare feet, just shave the grass

Friendships these days have an expiration date,

Honesty and lies debate,

But behind every lie an experience

It builds your mind up, making you look bright and great.

Self-esteem deserves the reliance,

Raise your self-esteem rate.

Study your life lessons as science,

Life is only about tests and mistakes.

Tears and smiles alliance

Remember, your environment is who you are.

"SEEK FOR BETTER"

Every tear,
Every fear
It hides behind your strength.
Every day,
Every year,
A chance to fix what we've made,
A chance to what we want,
A chance to fix our life grades
Creating bright colors for our shades
Getting higher and taller with the grieves
we weighed
Better construction with the desolation we
craved,
Because we can make our point of views
loud to be heard
Not only lawyers can persuade.
Pride can never be used for trade.
Personalities are victims for mistakes,
Improve it, well played.
Some personalities meant to ache
Under the power of fake
They say, "That's how we want it to be."
They got a sense of humor, for god sake,

And if earth had ears it would explode in laugh,
In the expression for earthquake
I pray for these sorts of people one day to awake.
Souls are released to break,
To be fixed again,
Even if they lost so many and they just can't,
There is a lesson behind every temporary friend.
Redeem your emotions till the end,
Lying to protect your feelings have been always a temporary shelter,
Which leads to brain welter,
Goals are meant to extend.
Show them how smallest messages can be send.
Every minor crack in the mirror,
Every minor crack in the moment
Will find a way to amend.
Remember, to follow it in your own direction.

"WHAT IF LIFE WAS FROM OUR IMAGINATION"?

What if life was a dream?
And our smiles were thoughts?
Our goals were a theme?
Love was a scheme?
Silence is our screams,
Mistakes will redeem,
But at the end nothing look like what it seems.
What if life was an illusion?
Our sorrows found a conclusion?
Kept Feelings has escaped the diffusion?
A dead soul has found a transfusion?
Broken hearts got healed; yes it was only a contusion?
What if life was a fantasy?
And our cries were a symphony?
Piano and violin
Injuries were phony as tattoos.
We were born with a pure skin.
We seek for mistakes it's not authorized,
We should differentiate between them and a sin.
We could get a chance

Winners don't necessarily win.
We don't need to use only feet steps to dance,
We don't always get a brief from a glance,
Creative people were not born an advance.
Love isn't only a romance.
Nothing has an end to enhance.

"3AM GLASS"

It's the moment when you feel starving,
But your tommy is already full of grudges.
Stones are craving
A shape of a desire
It's the moment where the walls are closing,
And for pain you're dosing.
Trying to put you back together,
But you have swallowed every piece in you,
But it took forever,
So there's a missing pieces and you just feel
lost.
Every time you laugh you feel clever,
For finding a gate to escape,
But you keep getting back to where you
were,
Yeah the maze has a circular shape
And for happy moments you wish you could
find a glance of tape,
So cold to pretend
When you were the worst actor,
You're afraid of your friends,
Not a step closer, don't even recommend.
For a grief you depend,

Life lessons to attend,
Elastic fake smiles to extend,
From joy school a paper of a suspend,
For prayers you've bend.

"I LET YOU IN"

I never trusted anyone but I let in my
imperfection
You felt shallow when you've seen my
depths,
So you left it unfold
I wanted you to get deeper in me,
But you fear heights; you're just not bold.
I don't breath you anymore I smoke you,
It's Bad for my lungs,
Or I breathe you not as oxygen but as a
carbon dioxide,
That's how I warm my frizzing tongue
It's still not healthy and I'm too young.
I only asked for a shelter, but the shelter was
my shadow.
When I see flares I remember you, because
they rarely fall
Just like you rarely exist.
When you do I wish I could resist,
But it's hard on my wrist.
Don't get me wrong you're the only thing I
really miss.
The love you gave me is so fragile

My life without you is so straggly.
They say, "Before you fall asleep you start to imagine things you would wish for it to happen."
That's when I wished for you to be close,
And every night I'm squeezing my bed sheets.
Your laugh is what I overdose
Lots of unsaid word yet, I don't feel complete
The way your voice puts me in a comatose,
But why do I still feel I'm on the streets
When I should have been home?
But I let you in when I thought I lost the key
When I thought that I locked my trust away.
One day you're a thrill,
The other day you make me suffer
Is that a way to make me pay the bill?

"We can build an empire"

The beauty behind the bleach,
A rainbow have lined our lives to reach,
Rules are defined for us in breach,
Glamour behind your every aggressive speech,
We get crashed for each other's to also teach.
In my whole life I have never seen
How flaws structured your perfectness.
You always glance replying, "What do you mean?"
Your dust is the sparkle of our memory scenes.
Our nature is always blue, never green.
The feelings of invisible crown, yet a queen.
I showed clear symptoms of an infection,
Too late for a vaccine
On the peak never between
Everything is fragile,
Only when you're not holding it tight,
So just be the light,
The light of my gloomy nights
We have so many reasons to fight,

Even the doubters have cleared our way.
We have tried the wrong to conclude with what's right.
I'll be every bite in your delight,
But promise to be my knight.
I'll be the ladder to the heights,
But don't let me freeze without firelight,
I'll always read your name letters in the word home.
I only understood how to be alone,
Without you
In a desert full of stones,
I'll be the rose.
I know everything feels hard,
But that's how life goes.
We can dig for real behind the curtains,
Hold my hand to ruin these shows.
Actors are fake let's work it to the expose,
Because only god knows
How I'm able to break every head till the toes
To any insurgent to our empire
Ready to set fire,
Provide me with power,
And be the infinity wire.

"OUT OF WORDS"

When your pride loses it definition,

When your legs aren't in stable position,

Your heart shakes in addition,

Feelings out of tradition,

Mixed emotions competition,

Looking left and right for recognition,

That's how does it feels like to fall deeply,

Fall deeply inside a hole with no way out.

Sliding so fast, into you so steeply,

Thoughts with no fears and doubts,

Finding for poems a subject to write about.

Without you, gardens live in hard season of drought,

And everyone can easily notice,

If my smiled have crossed my face with no limits of lengths and widths,

It's because of you.
The person I became,

Your art

If I had an appearance of pale colors,

It's because of you.

And if I today woke up with spectrum covering my body,

It's because of you.

If I ever mentioned number it would always be two,

Me and you

As homeless as I sound,

It's when you're not around

And if I could describe you in words

They're left in the silence.

I always wished to escape the reality for a while,

But I only stayed because you lived there.
It feels delightful finding a murder to strangle me with joy.

"PRECIOUS VALUE"

My dreams felt like burning,

But hey you

You are my solid ground.

You made it real by just being around

All the paths seemed dull

And you're the chandelier that I found.

To my fantasy illusions,

You are the symphony sound.

You make me want to race Shakespeare,

Trying to destroy his legacy.

Leaving a trace of you here,

The beautiful violin to my ear,

You can match the isolated politics,

You have the smile with the sweetest charm.

You made magic exist with your tricks,

The solution to every conflict and kicks,

You fell from heaven and turned my life into paradise.

You turned everything with your morals into cheap price.

You hunted my mind and distracted it,

Made me hard to notice anything, a simple sacrifice.

You make me smile even when you criticize,

Words just not enough for what is really on the inside

I swallowed my pride.

"UNITED"

She was lying on the beach shore

They told her, "Life would take something in order to give more."

And in every drifting wave,

She asked, "Whom will she live for?"

Until the eyes of that someone merged with stars.

He was waiting for life to knock her down in order to open his door.

She felt nothing like this before,

Her emotions started to pour,

Her body got buried beautifully underneath the sands.

He pulled her deeper with his strong hands,

In what she was drowning, she couldn't understand.

Her heart authority was giving her a command,

It wasn't even a choice.

She was following someone's voice,

It was too close like her-own shadow.

The bridges that blocked her way,

She was finally able to cross through.

She had nothing, but her soul that is left for her to pay,

And when the voice have started to disappear,

She screamed and said, "Stay,

Without you, I'm like breathing clay

That is breathing nothing.

I'm ready to drown to discover you,

I have nothing to lose anyway.

I've crossed all my life and I'm still in the halfway."

And that decision have changed her life

She became the ignited bones in December nights.

She had her smile on, every time she writes.

And every time she dive in midnights,

She was the light.

She never needed a law to prove that she was right.

She never craved anything after that night,

She had a locked appetite.

She saw behind her pale past a delight,

And believed them when they said, "Behind a storm a rainbow."

Because of that knight,

He held her tight.

For her, he took every poisoned bite.

She was his firelight in the North Pole.

She was his diamond in a cave filled with coals.

She was the plan to his goals.

She filled his organs with a soul.

To each other's, they took the role,

Like they were one.

Together they took control, Control of everything.

"CROWDED PLACE"

The colors are fading
And I'm still waiting.
It's turning black and white
You've took away the light
Leaving me alone in this fight.
I don't want to risk you,
That's why I'm fighting my mind.
Without you I've lost my vision
And I'm blind.
I'm sick of remembering memories,
Trying to use you as a remedy,
But nothing can work out from one side.
I rather suicide than lifted out in cries,
Don't you know how much I've died?
I've been screaming in the mind, killed in
the heart and hanging out with the silence.
That's what I kept inside,
Why am I here?
Why am I drunk in tears?
Feeling that I'm used for fun.
Your voice chases me every time I try to run.
It feels like there's no place for me in this
crowd,

I tried to tell you this in whispers,
I tried to tell you this out loud,
But you weren't even near and for this love
I bleed,
And by salty tears that myself feeds.
Tell me whether I stay or leave?

"IT USED TO BE A MYSTERY"

Words collision with no way out.

Being certain of everything inside you, no doubt.

When a river is water satisfied with no drought.

A warrior, because every second I survive,

I survive a brain stroke whenever I think of you.

Not every road needs licenses to drive

You just suddenly arrive

To another destination with depth and heights,

And you either float or dive.

Both actions are beautiful,

When you dive you feel deadly in love,

And when you float you just feel alive.

Another way to pass,

You'll feel smart,

Because you'll understand what is used to be a mystery

Not only Romeo and Juliet history,

So is poetry...

Poetry will always hide a beauty,

Only when we're genius to figure out behind whom,

As the beauty of a garden bloom,

Emotions to consume,

As the shiny stars in a gloom

What are those eyes?

A perfect present filled with a surprise,

And in those eyes...

It holds a future inside.

"Frost"

When your home structure is a glass

Every time it breaks it never gets to the way it used to be.

When your mirror reflection has a crack,

And I see myself in you my other half.

Skeptical to love believes,

While yesterday it felt like a fact,

Something that can never change

Wondering if your emotions are fake or exact

Of what movies talk about?

Is the remedy a rearrange?

But now I know that silence can be heard in echoes.

The feelings of cracked pieces are not that strange.

I got drown in the depth of you,

You stood on the boat watching

No hands to pull me from out there.
And if you asked how's the life with me?

I'll say, "One day I can swim to you,

The next day I drown without you.

One day the waves drift me to you,

The next day wind makes the waves hard to resist

Taking me to the opposite direction from you.

And if I gave you control we would have never felt this.

Strange to love with not even clue

A lot of the memories I made for us would be missed."

You're busy of thinking that I want the impossible things,

While in the other hand I'll be on the other side

Expecting the simple things.

Maybe that's why everything we have lost is so hard to identify.

The winter came and instead our warmth has frosted.

Who and whom will accost?

When pride is the answer and it already has took over.

"CHANGE"

Like the heat of the sun
One day, it provides your body warmth.
The next day you get burned.
Like the shot of a gun
One day it saves you,
The next day it might kill you,
And you're just done.
Long way to run
From something used to be fun
Honesty ignited flames,
But we're hiding behind an ice burg.
The truth became lame,
And we're just frozen.
For who we are, we're just ashamed.
We wear excuses,
Honesty is you being naked.
We tried but our organs refuses,
We feel scared,
So our bombs defuse,
Fake smiles we reuse,
And when they find out
We end up with nothing to lose.
They say dance like nobody is watching,

But all what they hear are slow songs.
They say sing like nobody is going to hear you,
But the echoes were much louder than their vocal cords.
Exposing their talents is hard to afford,
People with fortune left on board,
While the real talents are waving at the seashore
Hard to believe stories,
Hard to believe king Arthur with the sword
They have to reveal their bodies to not be ignored,
Hide whom they are to get reward.
They never felt comfortable,
Until they lean toward the lord.
Since then, everything has started to change.
The light visualized their brains,
Smiles with no touch of lies stain.
The only tears they have felt are joy, or drops of rain.
Their previous past became lessons to gain.

"Definition by the Cover"

Black and white
It does not clarify your rights,
And whom you should be sitting beside.
Short or long
It does not navigate where you belong,
And height does not tell if you're strong
Or not...
You cannot tell me who to be,
Because love has no category,
And history does not define the future.
We can create a new story
It could be a battle of peace,
Art of glory
Nor blood desire no leaving souls,
Colorful smiles, tears inhibitory
Why do we care about our family history?
The members are in front of our eyes.
They tell us, "You shouldn't be walking with
this tribe.
It's not ours, it's not you and it's not us."
We haven't met, but that's how they describe,
And you can't even discuss
It's like it's a minus and plus,

But they forget how strong the attraction is,
And how together we could invent bliss.
No skin color can decide how to paint our tomorrows.
No names get to decide how to beat our sorrows.
And no genders get to decide what major should we borrow.
We were born with the same body cells
Embrace what you came in this life with
Instead of hiding under shells
Thousands of judgment they tell,
But I get to splash how my name smells.
Step right on your insults,
That's how I pay your words bell.

"STEADY FLIGHT"

We took a ride in this flight
Everything was filled with doubts,
But I was sure that without you my life is
never right.
A reason for me to try, continue and fight
Yes, beginning always shape slight.
It wasn't easy for me,
Wasn't easy to reach your heart,
But I decided to set my soul free,
And change the values in the chart.
Life is filled with lessons to see,
Yet I knew you from the start
That you were never a one
You never left any trace,
Because you ended up to be life,
You ended up as a grace.
Changed my whole world,
You're filled with challenges and I'm ready
to race.
I just can't give up your face.
I used to be impartial,
A different case when it comes to you.
I know life with me is filled with turbulence,

And our transportation isn't stable,
But our passion together is shapeable,
And real.
I can see our destination clearly.
A little while more
And our plane will land.
Our haters will get band.
Our powerful reunited hand.
Negativity expand,
Show them how do we stand.

"WINTER NIGHTS IN JULY"

My friends told me once,
"The more we suffer the better it is,
The longer it takes the better it taste."
And I waited,
For fine I faked it.
Memories started to take place.
Reality started to split,
Crowded social life with no place for me
to sit.
Having someone constantly, habitual
This dope is so hard to quit.
Doing you like a religious ritual.
Gloomy mirror, oh dear my other half is
missing.
I never believed in fiction,
Till the sound of your ghost hissing
It's getting cold in here and I don't know
why am I sitting away from the heater,
Yet I forgot it was you.
I hate being away for even a meter,
And for the past years I'm looking for the
repeater.
You inspire my demons to write about.

You're the one my lines can't exist without,
But lately with you my happiness became
a doubt.
So, ignite my heart it beats numb without you.
Those lines keep whispering too.
Even when your broken lights have driven
me to darkness,
Let's try candles.
The door is locked,
But you can be the key and I can be the
handle,
Open me.
I rather to hide my secrets under a shell
Than to let people steal my precious pearl.
But I got your back in my depths steal me.
I'll catch you when you fall into it.
I hate simulations, but I can't stop pretending
that I'm fine.
Counting till 10 calming my sorrow,
Hold me closer when I reach nine.
Don't live in yesterday be my graceful
tomorrow.
They said, "Fairytales couldn't be true."
I wish you were not a one.
Eyes so red itching for your beautiful view.
You killed me,
And lifted this crime with no clue,

No clue to be found.
Lips are blue,
Freezing nights
Craving your warmth.

"Isolation"

An old wound keeps bleeding from times to times,

But I love the bandage after your beautiful crimes

The way you precede there isn't a better sublime.

I don't want to be an open book.

I'm an expensive pearl. But you stole the whole shell.

You structure my body just like a cell.

Every organ consist you.

Without you I'm lost with nothing to do.

All I know is that I'll walk on your shoe

Whenever your legs are broken.

I want to define you, but the words resist to be spoken.

I'll be your brain whenever your thoughts split.

I'll be your sweater on a winter nights when nothing fits.

And if I get to choose what would I be, I'll be the air the passes your path, slap your cheeks,

Because I know the righteous ways, beside you I know how to climb the peaks.

In extraterrestrial space you're the plant that I would land on, survive on.

Love had proved me a theory with a phenomenon.

So, ignite me till I'm numb.

Hold me till I'm unconscious.

Drown me till the end of a plumb.

I'll be your china doll.

Hold me so tight,

Isolate my soul.

Show me your flaws, despite any bright.

For you, I would surround myself.

For you, I would daily fight.

My waterproof stain, how can something ruin my skin, turn into a cure?

"No and not"

No equipment,

No hands,

but yet your love is strangling me,

That I might proceed to the next degree,

Where there are no limits,

Neither oceans nor seas,

But yet your love is drowning me to the seafloor.

It's hard to think about my goals when you're hunting my mind.

People telling me "This is too much, what are you sacrificing for?"

But I've never felt this way before.

I give to life to gain more,

And I know more is all about you.

With you my chemicals know how to pour,

And I need to instruct them.

No remedy for this beautiful sore.

You're so beautiful that you irritate every single broken piece.

The magical thoughts you release,

What kind of tools they have been using because you're a masterpiece.

And whenever you walk,

You caused my skin itches and crease.

And your pupils shine crystal clear,

Ending up drying my tears.

I'm locked in a sphere.

I'm rolling over your zone.

The angels and devils in a relationship,

Never believed that, but you made it appear

You have weaken every organ in me that used to be so intense, so severe.

Not a heaven nor hell,

But this miracle in a collision with curse.

"RELEASED"

When the cover smile goes naked,
When the doubts prove their bright side,
When you freeze and that feeling goes
snaked,
It's hard to explain it, but you know it's
modified.
I'm skeptical to feeling safe, but not on your
side.
Even if being with you lead me to walking
on thorns,
That's where I would blindly decide,
Because in the depth of my smile, your
reflection.
It's like you and paradise are on the same
direction.
Even if it was an infection,
Leave me uncured.
And if someone mentioned your name it
would goes under temptation, allured.
So, darling, take it out on me.
I'm your glass whenever you need to
break one.
If your lights went off I'll be your sun.

I'll be your racetrack whenever you need
to run.
I'll redeem your heart when it's undone.
And if you ever wondered why it's only you,
Because every time I try to deny the fact
that you're my home
The sky starts to rain and I found myself
stuck inside,
Because when I'm alone without you I rather
suicide,
Because spontaneously I always put my
sorrows on the side whenever you asked to
fight yours,
Because for my illness you're the only cure,
Because you alarm my coldness,
Because you're the sweet taste of boldness,
Yet every time we try to walk a distance
further our souls find a way back right
beside each other.
So, every time you touch my heart remind
yourself to never stop.
The beat sound noisy if we're apart.
And I know in your love I heavily flop,
Ignite my soul and burn it badly.
Show me love don't show me mercy,
That's where I know I'm on the top
Remind yourself to never stop.

I don't know how to sugar coat with words, but I know I have the heart that is able to ache in order to see your smile in rewinding process.

"A GOOD REASON"

A skipped question
Feelings have frozen
The thoughts had a lack of digestion.
I know what I have chosen,
But the future bites
Where past collides,
And you on my side
Kills me thousands of times
And I feel terrified.
Between reality and our dreams,
Lots of solutions my brain hides.
Between the joy and the fears,
Your eyes make me hypnotized.
Hold my hand strongly,
And tell me it's a period of time.
Hold tight into everything
And tell me that we don't deserve a fine.
So close to the top, yet so far,
A rough mountain to climb
Where it levels hurts
And shows the worst words rhyme.
Seconds are wasted,
We could have lived the best times.

What a gap!
Tomorrows are on this lap
Where sitting on it feels like thorns,
But seeing your smile is a good reason to why I was born.
I have no doubts towards you
And I know what to do
Hope it's good enough,
Good enough to make the future easy to see through.

"SOMETHING TRUE"

A billion questions
With one answer, no hesitations
Two hearts nation
A great amount of power,
They don't need any explanation.
Love symptoms were the same,
Through the personality variations
They found in both of their eyes a light
Since then, they knew they were living in the
dark.
When they were apart,
There souls were filled with sparks.
And when the ocean waves drift apart,
They rather sink with the sharks.
She is strangled with a rope.
She is strangled with this.
She loves how does it feels, daily dope,
Yet she hopes
She gets strangled harder
Till her skin turns blue,

Because she's all over you
Everyone turned blur,
Because you're her only view
She finally felt something true.

"THEY DON'T UNDERSTAND"

Two minds,
One nation,
One similar type of feeling,
Recording their own information
Everything was clear to everyone,
They didn't need any presentation.
Two hearts
United as one.
They didn't understand the importance of
time together.
They lived in a night where's there's a sun,
And a daylight where there is a moon.
As the bullet never came from a violent gun,
They gave up their lives for each other's,
As the bullet was a remedy
To everyone, they lived cold as ice.
To one another, hot as flames.
Their strength knew nothing with a price.
Throwing their souls for sacrifice
Everyone called them insanity,
So they asked them, "Are both of you okay?"

Their smiles had the reflection of each other's,
It's like they were living in paradise.
They said, "We live once for life,
For this kind of feeling we live twice."

SOMEONE YOU'LL ENJOY

Beyond the stars,
Way too far
That no one can reach
Even with a sport car
I captured those eyes.
My skin used to have the tone of bleach,
But I turned into a spectrum,
And that's where I want to be,
And that's where I rather be.
I got stuck in this jail of your picture
Seems like a home to me.
More like a mental disorder,
No cure but your shoulder.
Standing on insanity border
And I rather live there,
Because I found a fresh air
They say old is gold,
But you'll remain new.
Everything is blur expect your view,
And that's not a song
It's something to prove that I was living wrong,
It's something to be settled in for long.

Not hope but a dream.
I'm just hoping that everything is like what
it seems.
Feelings in a cobweb,
But the map has one target,
And I'm ready for the mess,
Ready for the green button to press.
What's success without a thousand stresses?
I know I have flaws,
But I promise to redress.
I know the glass will break behind you,
But the joy will pour.
A value to suffer for
My inner parts are filled with dust,
But there's a beauty behind the things we
store.
The dark waves seem terrifying,
But the dawn holds the beauty of the
seashore.
You'll never feel bored
I'm someone to explore.
From you, I want more.

MISUNDERSTOOD

I asked you once, "What have you found in me so differently?"
You preached in silence.
I smiled in tears,
The answer was hard like science,
Since that day I had a lack of confidence.
My organs were uglier than ever.
My demons found a way to be clever.
I felt ugly,
But the surprise was that I am too pretty,
That you lacked words and I didn't knew this yet.
I felt petty,
But another surprise was that you were drowning in my depths, yet you're fighting to breath.
It feels like my heartbeats are beating in black,
But you wanted to tell me in every pulse that I was too kind that the angels had a walk of shame when they pass by.
You couldn't,
Because I was a full biology book,

In every organ I damaged, you still love to
meditate them.
Because I was a full book of chemistry,
I was behind every shiver and butterfly in
your tummy.
Because I was a full physics book,
When I covered my face with both of my
hands
You took my hands off telling me
"I want to look."
I thought you were searching for flaws.
I scratched the mirror with my claws,
And when you saw the mirror
You opened up your jaw.
You said,
"Your question will steal every second
moving by the clockwise.
And every time I look at you I rise.
It's hard to talk about something I always
utilize.
Me leaning that is what I find in your eyes.
It's so difficult to talk about you in words,
Because they will never put me in satisfy.
Using words for you is criticism.
You're not a regular organism.
I settled with you, it could be nationalism.
When you asked me I found a flock of
reasons,

I got trapped and couldn't find my way out.
I know I put you into doubts
Just know if one day I answered your question,
Then my feelings are never true,
Because true feelings makes you lost,
Plus without I lose myself."

IMMORTALITY

Uncoil your thoughts,
Steal the time.
You'll never get caught.
Counterclockwise your past,
Don't stick with the rules.
Walk your seconds like a turtle steps.
Be the creativity hidden behind the moment,
Things won't last when it goes fast.
Draw your fingerprint.
Act like your wide open,
While you're only giving hints
I know there are times where we laughed
While we actually didn't
Don't be a flare on daylights,
They don't shine.
Enhance your crystalline.
Never show an oblique spine.
Make your moments hard to define.
We were born to discover,
Search where you belong.
Reach to your goals don't just hover,
Be the material not the shallow cover.

Twist every insult hurts you; you'll get the actual meaning.
Haters are our secret lovers.
Paint your waterproof colors.
Embrace your personality,
Be the originality.
Don't be someone who is created artificiality.
Walk your steps through immortality.

TO MY READERS...

In our lives we have something we call it
fails and the opposite, which is successes
they pretty much seem different to you all,
but if you have looked behind the letters
They look approximately the same,
How?
Fails are actually the path way to success,
so they both make you reach the same goal.
However the much we fail the closer we are
to what we have dreamed of.
Fails are also the synonym for lessons. So,
the more we fail the more we learn, the
more we grow and the more we rise.
My story basically I'm the one who failed
a dozen of times, and yes I have reached
the state where I wanted to give up, where
I wanted to rush in tears, where I thought
I was a loser and where I wished I was
someone else. Yet, I have gathered every
piece of myself together and merged it to a
different picture, a different me and stronger
person.

I started writing since I was a 12 years old kid. Then, day-by-day I found myself getting deeper, week-by-week I found myself merging with lines and colliding with the surrounding environment inventing what I brought to you.

I interacted with everything; the books, movies, nature, the dawns, love novels, music and mistakes.

We were all born with an art, it was not made for specific people, we were all born talented with a duty in this world.

We all have a department in art that we can find it hidden behind our feelings and everything we pass by.

Yes, everything I passed by even others experiences I take a use of it and create lines as an output from it.

I saw how people we're interested in Shakespeare mostly love poetries even though he died. And I wanted to be immortal just like him. That's why I named the book immortality.